MOTIVATIONAL POETIC VERSES

Gary G. Tavares

MOTIVATIONAL POETIC VERSES

Printed in the United States of America by KDP

Cover graphics by Richard Anthony Evans

Published by Tavares Entertainment, LLC.:

Gary G. Tavares

Tavares Entertainment, LLC.

3320 S. Cobb Dr.SE Unit H-21

Smyrna, GA 30080

678-437-4496

www.tavaresentertainment.com

ISBN: 979-8-218-79886-4

A WRITER'S VIEWPOINT

It's the first day of the rest of my life.
I'm over 60 with one son and no wife.
To become a well-known writer is my goal.
I'll work at it until I'm one hundred years old.

I'm trying to be another famous Tavares.
Many years ago, I decided to start this.
Not like the musical Tavares group of the past.
They were extremely talented but did not last.

I ask what my steps to achieving it are.
No matter what happens, I've already come far.
Writing is what I love to do.
Films, plays, books and poetry too.

Just see my work is all I request.

Please don't let it sit on your desk.

Much worse don't put it in the round file.

Agents, please listen I know your style.

Letting my pen flow ever so freely.

It's not so easy you have to believe me.

Sitting here looking towards the ceiling.

Trying to give these poems lots of feeling.

I'm a Writer that holds more than one title.

creating original works is also vital.

I'll give my advice to writers in this poem.

If you get rejected, you just have to show 'em.

Don't let anyone destroy your dream.

Just keep pursuing it and you'll see what I mean.

BATTERED AND BRUISED

You're trying your best to hide your bruises.
He slaps you around and says that you're useless.
You're starting to believe that maybe it's true.
He doesn't appreciate anything you do.

Make-up hides bruises but not the pain.
There's little sunshine and lots of rain.
It's like you're on a roller coaster ride.
With Doctor Jekyll and Mister Hyde.

Love should never include pain.
But for you he has so much disdain.
You say it's hard for you to get out.
Could it be yourself who you really doubt?

Being beat by him is not amusing.

He tells you he loves you but it's you he's confusing.

Everyone wonders why you keep on staying.

You'll get out safely we're hoping and praying.

He keeps getting worse and acting really strange.

When will you realize he's not going to change?

The verbal abuse is just as bad.

It tears you down and keeps you sad.

It makes you feel like less than a lady.

And sometimes it even makes you feel crazy.

What he did to you was assault and battery.

You keep on saying, "Oh he's just mad at me."

You keep on believing that it's your fault.

And you keep on taking his assault.

The police come so often your home is their substation.

You never press charges, so it causes frustration.

Sad thing is he too was a victim.

But I refuse to make excuses for him.

Just look at your face in the mirror.

Old bruises new bruises but it never gets clearer.

Sometimes he treats you like you're a Queen.

But what about the times he's just plain mean?

You long for the times he treats you right.

You're hoping and praying for another good night.

Please get out of this for heaven's sake.

If you don't, you're making a big mistake.

When all is said and done it's your decision.

Getting out should be your primary mission.

You thought he was the best man in the world.

But you made a mistake so move on girl!

CHILD OF THE GHETTO

Born a beautiful child with dark brown skin.
But my life was rough so where do I begin?
My daddy left me when I was two.
I became a Thug, what else could I do?

Destined to lose right out the gate.
My life was filled with anger and hate.
My mother did the best she could.
But it was really tough in my neighborhood.

My only role models were pimps and thugs.
At fourteen years old I took two slugs.
I decided education was not for me.
I never knew what I wanted to be.

Gary G. Tavares

By fifteen I decided to leave home.
I was very scared and all alone.
With no skills how would I survive?
I couldn't get no nine-to-five!

I started hanging out with the wrong crowd.
But robbin' and stealin' didn't make me proud.
Drugs and alcohol helped me with my pain.
There was never sunlight always rain.

I spent some of my youth incarcerated.
Society's monster was now created.
I began to realize that crime wasn't paying.
I wanted to change; you see what I'm saying?

The last time I was released from prison.
I knew I had to make the right decision.
I finished school and got my education
Staying out of trouble took hard work and dedication.

My mother once said to never let go.

Just because you were born a "Child of the Ghetto."

DOPE BOY

You're selling drugs to your own people.

You're like a terrorist bomb but twice as lethal.

Do you really think it's a lasting career?

You blame the man but it's you we all fear!

You say that you're making plenty of cash.

But are you willing to die for your poisonous stash?

You have so many excuses for destroying the community.

But you're part of the reason that there is no unity.

You think you're taking the easy way out.

You'll be dead or in prison without a doubt.

I know you understand exactly what I'm saying.

I at least got you thinking I'm hoping and praying.

It's time to start thinking BEFORE you act.
If you make the wrong decision, there's no turning back.
What happened to your desire to be successful?
Your line of work is way too stressful!

Worrying about getting robbed, killed or busted.
Your friends and clients can never be trusted.
Is this a skill you would teach to your children?
The revolving door would turn again and again.

Drug dealing skills passed generation to generation.
Causing widespread neighborhood and community deterioration.
You say, "I have to do what I have to do!"
But what are you going to do when they come for you?

Yes, eventually you will be caught.
You were so untouchable at least you once thought.
Is Drug Dealer a title you hold with pride?
So, what you have cash, gold and a nice ride!

Everything you own can be gone in an instant.

Now you're incarcerated wanting to repent.

Being successful can bring lots of joy.

But you'll never be successful being a "Dope Boy."

GANG BANGER

You seek acceptance from a posse of thugs.
You have done everything with them including sell drugs.
You're fighting for streets that aren't even yours.
Many friends are gone from all the wars.

These are wars that can't be won.
Can anyone remain standing when all is said and done?
The cycle of violence never ends.
Sooner or later, you'll run out of friends.

Do you really believe that they are your friends?
You look at me and say, "Well that all depends."
Would they visit you if you were incarcerated?
Their true allegiance to you would be demonstrated.

When you're incarcerated you will be on your own.
They won't even call you on the telephone!
If you were killed, they wouldn't even pay their respects.
You can see how much loyalty for you that reflects!

They would pour out some liquor for their fallen comrade.
You truly have potential so it would really be sad.
Listen to these words from an educated Poet.
I'm telling the truth, and I am sure that you know it.

Yesterday your Posse took out someone's brother.
You said, "Well he shouldn't have worn the wrong color!"
Maybe they took him out for being in your hood.
Whatever the reason it was definitely not good.

It's so easy for you to take someone out.
But you don't even know what life is about.
If you want a war, you can join the Army.
Go to Iraq and be all you can be!

Get out of the gang before it's too late.

Even if you have to move from your state.

You say you're hoping to be around for a while.

I suggest you give up that "Gang Banger" lifestyle.

NON-FUNCTIONING ALCOHOLIC TEEN

You drank last night you have a headache to remind you.
You're thanking God that the night's behind you.
You're bowing down before the Porcelain Goddess.
But you missed this time just look at the mess!

The room keeps spinning you just want it stopped.
It was your decision to drink 'til you dropped.
You roll over again and hit the snooze.
How many school days do you plan to lose?

You drink so much your grades are dropping.
It's really time to think about stopping.
Telling your friends you're not an alcoholic.
But you drink like a fish what else can you call it?

Look at you stumble all over the place.

It's a crying shame and such a disgrace.

You're just slowly killing yourself.

Put that bottle back on the store shelf!

You might as well put a gun to your head.

There's no more pain 'cause now you're dead.

Your speech is slurred and you're acting ignorant.

You want to fight and you're getting belligerent.

I see that you're really just thinking of you.

But your family and friends are quite concerned too.

Teenage drinking is at an all-time high.

The statistics could make a grown man cry.

Do you know what alcohol does to you?

It will make you look like you're one hundred and two.

It tears you down from the inside out.

Eventually killing you without a doubt.

To make things worse you're not twenty-one.
You're breaking the law but to you that's fun.
You never said, "When I grow up, I want to be a bum."
But at this rate that's exactly what you'll become.

You treat that bottle like it's some sort of savior.
Pour out that liquor and do yourself a favor!
You may have even driven drunk in the past.
It won't be joy riding if you get in a crash!

Now you're faced with a DUI.
You can kiss that driver's license good-bye.
Worse yet you could end up in jail.
Now you're a felon destined to fail.

If you live your life would be changed forever.
The tragedy is that you really knew better.
So before getting wasted just stop and think.
Do I really need to take this drink?

I'm hoping that you make the right decision.

Try a new hobby like maybe fishin.'

You'll be much better in the long run.

It's true life is challenging but it's also fun.

RISKY BEHAVIOR: UNPROTECTED SEX

HIV has been around for a while.
You have unprotected sex like it's going out of style.
Eventually you are going to get stuck.
You'll play Russian roulette and run out of luck!

To utilize a condom is simple and easy.
She said, "When you use those things you just don't please me."
You have multiple partners and never use protection.
You say, "I don't like condoms they mess with my erection."

You still believe it's just a gay disease.
Get educated about HIV please!
It also affects straight males and females.
Let's educate communities and increase condom sales!

Many of the newly infected happen to be teens.

Do you all understand what abstinence means?

It's not just at-risk groups that can be infected.

It can be anyone who is not protected.

You come up with that senseless and ridiculous line.

"They look pretty healthy, and they appear to be fine."

Your partner may not look infected.

Be sure that a trusted condom is always selected.

Get yourself tested regularly.

That is the responsibility of you and me.

Have your partner tested too.

Tell them it's something they have to do.

Abstinence is the only sure way.

But use a condom if you have to play!

Do yourself and everyone else a favor.

Refrain from this type of "Risky behavior."

SAGGY STYLE

It's time for our youth to take a stance.
They can start by simply pulling up their pants.
Yes, saggy pants have been here a while.
Perhaps it's time to try a new style.

You wonder why you can't get a job.
It's that much harder if you look like a slob.
It's a style that came straight out of prison.
It's not you but the style that I'm dissin.'

I know you'll say that you don't care.
But folks are tired of looking at your underwear!
Much worse you're constantly showing your behind.
If you think that's cute you've lost your mind.

You do it because everyone else is doing it.

You can't be different just a little bit?

Just who are you really trying to impress?

You're walking around looking a mess.

You're pulling up your pants every step you take.

At least use a belt for heaven's sake!

All you have to do is look in the mirror.

What I'm saying to you would become much clearer.

Your pants are so low that you can't even run.

But they work really well for concealing a gun.

These words of advice are for the women too.

Your saggy pants just aren't cute boo!

Judging you is not my intention.

This is something I needed to mention.

So pulling up your pants could be worth while.

Now you've created your own funky style.

LITTLE AND BAD: THE SCHOOL BULLY

You intimidate others and control them with fear.
You are not likely to become the student of the year!
You physically assaulted another student.
Do you really believe that your actions were prudent?

You made a student feel like less than a person.
Your destructive behavior continues to worsen.
Instilling fear in others seems to empower you.
Can you go without bullying for an hour or two?

What goes around will eventually come back around.
Now just listen for a minute and do not make a sound!
One day you will inevitably meet your match.
If so, let your own medicine flow down your hatch!

It is never right to assault someone.

To you, assaulting others is lots of fun.

Have you heard the biblical saying that starts with, "Do unto others?"

You should treat them as if they were your sisters or brothers!

Perhaps you have an anger control problem.

You may have other problems, but your behavior will not solve them.

Perhaps belittling others makes you feel bigger.

You need to think about all the misery you trigger.

Perhaps you think bullying will give you respect.

You could care less about the people whose lives you affect.

Some of your victims will develop long-term issues.

Your verbal assault and teasing are worse than a bruise.

You think you are so big and tough, which is extremely sad.

However, you are "The school bully," which means you are just "Little and bad."

SKY HIGH

Drugs are no good you're living a lie.
Are you giving up on life and ready to die?
It doesn't matter which drug you choose.
It still could end up the one you abuse.

Life is rough and sometimes you slip.
But drugs will take you on a one-way trip!
You're still saying, "Marijuana isn't harmful."
But deep inside you know that's bull!

It makes you paranoid and quite forgetful.
You did something stupid and now you're regretful.
You're feeling strong and you're feeling bold.
Is getting high your only goal?

Perhaps you're dealing with more than one problem.

No matter how bad they are drugs won't solve them.

The list of illegal drugs is long and dreadful.

What they can do to you is really incredible.

Marijuana, Meth and of course Cocaine.

Those are a few drugs that mess up your brain.

Some legal drugs can also be addictive.

Stop popping pills like you don't want to live.

They're called over the counter and prescription.

Have you read their label and their description?

Don't let life pass you by.

Enjoy it to the fullest and stop getting high!

A PLEDGE TO SAVE OUR YOUTH

Today we embark on uncharted waters.
We pledge to be better parents to our sons and daughters.
They are our future, and we pretty much know it.
You say you're concerned but you don't seem to show it.

We must save them and narrow the generation gap.
The responsibility falls in everyone's lap.
It all starts with parenting and education.
Get involved because they need your dedication.

Yes, it is time for us to get more involved.
It is the only way their problems can ever be solved.
So, I am speaking to you with these lines that rhyme.
More than anything else, they just need your time.

Young men, please do not continue to abandon your children.
Perhaps I need to reiterate this at least once again!
Unfortunately, there are too many fatherless households.
The neighborhood or community is the first thing that folds.

I believe each child needs a strong family.
I hope you're listening, and you really understand me.
Young women need to make better decisions before they become mothers.
Sadly, your father wasn't there, and your mother raised you and your brothers.

We can no longer ignore these problems or continue to hide.
We must instill in them some sense of pride.
You may believe that our youth are totally lost.
We can all just give up on them, but at what cost?

Parents, stop treating your child like a friend.

If you don't, their respect for you will fade like the wind.

We must rally to improve our educational system.

If we don't, the future of our children will continue to look grim.

Just hoping their problems will go away will not help their situation.

So, get involved and try making a difference is my only stipulation.

Deep inside, you know I am telling the truth.

Do your part and make, "A pledge to save our youth."

SMOKE SCREENS SHATTERED DREAMS

The school bathroom is filled with cigarette smoke.
Hold your breath or you'll surely choke.
Trying to be down with the rest of the crowd.
Smoking isn't cool for crying out loud!

You think smoking makes you mature?
It makes you smell bad sort of like horse manure.
Maybe it makes you feel like you're cool.
It's killing you slowly don't be such a fool.

The tobacco industry has done enough.
But they don't force you to take that puff!
Then when you're sick, you expect to get millions.
Those guys are smart they're not the silly ones!

Heart disease, lung disease and high blood pressure.

The long-term effects are hard to measure.

You smoke to have friends and feel like you're grown.

Perhaps you're better off just being alone.

Let's be real it's a terrible habit.

To make it worse you're young and new at it.

Do whatever it takes for you to quit.

You'll say, "I feel much better I have to admit."

Words of wisdom for me to part with.

Cigarette smoking don't even start it!

TEEN BABY MAMA

If I talked about boys, it became a heated discussion.
My parents said I'm too young and I'm rushin.'
My mom and dad were very protective.
A little too much from my perspective.

All I wanted was to have some fun.
I felt like a prisoner that was on the run.
At sixteen years old I felt I was grown.
I thought I was ready to be on my own.

I ran the streets and came home late.
It wasn't long before I started to date.
I met a guy who seemed really into me.
I even let him have my virginity.

I didn't force him to use protection.
I was really naïve and afraid of rejection.
I got pregnant which was no surprise.
He said it's not his baby and began telling lies.

I told my parents I was keeping the baby.
They said, "What's wrong with you girl have you gone crazy?"
They said, "Why bring a child into this world?"
"You're not grown yet you're just a little girl."

I ran away from home to get away for a while.
I was having sex like it was going out of style.
I ended up in a home for teen mothers.
I wasn't alone there were plenty of others.

I ran away again and my baby was taken.
I didn't realize the mistake I was making.
I ended up getting into prostitution and drugs.
I couldn't seem to stop meeting Thugs!

I almost died of a drug overdose.

It was like I saw a light that was ever so close.

I just needed to get my life in order.

I wanted to be the one raising my daughter.

I got some help and stayed clean and sober.

I got my baby back and I'll never let go of her.

I got her back but making it was tough.

The neighborhood we lived in was rather rough.

My daughter has a ten-year-old and she's only twenty-four.

Talk about turning a revolving door!

I had a life that was so full of drama.

Just because I became a "Teen baby mama."

THE "BLING-BLING" THING

You have a different car for every day of the week.
But for some reason it's happiness you still seek.
You love your big and beautiful home.
With acres of land for you to roam.

You have plenty of gold and diamonds galore.
Enough to start your own jewelry store.
You have lots of designer and customized clothes.
What an extravagant lifestyle you chose.

You're living the life of a Hollywood star.
But does the wealth change who you really are?
Living the life of the rich and the famous.
Feeling you're real big and no longer nameless.

Now folks come at you from everywhere.

On your way up none of them were there!

Now they come out of the woodwork.

It's enough to make you go berserk.

You have everything people only dream of.

But all your wealth can't buy you love.

So many women want you it's almost a joke.

You think they would be after you if you were still broke?

One of them wants to have the last laugh.

To be your wifey so they can claim half!

Who is your true friend and who is your foe?

For you it's like "eeny-meeny-miney-moe."

Money doesn't define who you really are.

Neither does having an expensive car.

Don't get me wrong being rich is a good thing.

But just remember you are not defined by your "bling-bling."

A MONTH OF HISTORY: THE MONTH OF FEBRUARY

February is a month of history.
I thank those who paved the way for me.
When I say to myself my job is challenging.
I remember the role of the honorable Doctor King.

A society that is totally free of discrimination.
How good that would be for this great nation.
Free of discrimination from race, gender, religion or creed.
This is important for us to succeed.

Although this nation has come a long way.
We are not quite there I would definitely say.
If we work together, we can do anything.
Just think of all the good it could bring.

I am trying to be the best in all that I do.

Staying out of trouble is okay too.

This month symbolizes peace and equality for all mankind.

A better goal is hard to find.

You can start by searching deep within your soul.

Just ask yourself how you can help achieve this goal.

It all starts with the person in the mirror.

It's really quite simple and couldn't be clearer.

The Pledge of Allegiance says with liberty and justice for all.

Without these freedoms our nation would fall.

What sacrifices are you willing to make?

We know plenty of diligence it will surely take.

To be judged by the content of your character not the color of
your skin. That's what we're all still fighting to win.
January fifteenth is not just a day off work or school.
To think of it as such is really not cool.

It's the birthday of the honorable Doctor King.
If you know of his contributions, it's a beautiful thing.
So, as I sit here and think about how fortunate I am.
I think of what others endured and say man oh man.

I think of those less fortunate than me.
We all know how bad the economy can be.
Let's not forget our soldiers in the Middle East.
War is not the answer so let's pray for peace.

Doctor King said hate can't drive out hate only love can.

So, let's try to love our fellow man.

He also said an eye for an eye leaves everyone blind.

It means don't retaliate just try to be kind.

To close this poem with a little disclaimer.

These are me and Doctor King's thoughts and that's a no brainer.

THE DISGRUNTLED PASSENGER

The bus is late, and it is starting to rain.
When the bus arrives, you'll be sure to complain.
The schedule said it would be there at eight.
Once again you are running real late.

You dial Customer service on your cellular phone.
There is no answer and you're feeling alone.
All you want is to hear a live person.
You can't get through and the rain starts to worsen.

You take out your umbrella, but it will not open.
It is bent out of shape and the button is broken.
Every other bus number arrives at that stop.
It will take some time for your blood pressure to drop.

At this point, you are starting to get nervous.
You begin to wonder if the bus is in service.
You have been splashed by several cars.
At the end of this ordeal, you'll be behind bars!

The bus finally comes but you have waited a while.
The driver opens the door and greets you with a smile.
You shout at the driver, "Where the hell have you been?"
"I don't particularly care for your stupid little grin!"

The driver said, "Sir I'm sorry for running behind.
But the rush hour traffic has been quite a grind."
You step on the bus all soaked and wet.
You want the driver to know that you're really upset.

You curse out the driver and create quite a scene.

You start to act ignorant, belligerent and mean.

The police arrive promptly and escort you off the bus.

There are things about that morning you need to discuss.

The Officer asked the driver, “Why did this occur?”

He said, “I was late, and he became a disgruntled passenger.”

A MEMORABLE CHRISTMAS EVE

It was a cold and dreary Christmas Eve.
The snow was deep so I couldn't leave.
I was alone in my house with my big Saint Bernard.
The weather was bad, or he would be in the yard.

I was feeling sad and a little down.
Most of my folks don't live in town.
I thought that maybe I could drive to see them.
Without a snowmobile that would be a problem.

If there is a will, there is certainly a way.
Perhaps I can see them by Christmas day.
I decided to turn on the television set.
There is nothing good on tonight I bet.

I turned to a Christmas flick for a minute.
It was so realistic that I felt I was in it.
I was feeling tired and was fading away.
I heard Santa outside with his reindeer and sleigh.

I got out of my seat and opened my door.
It was an amazing sight that I couldn't ignore.
Standing before me was old Saint Nick.
He looked like the Santa from the old Christmas flick.

He gestured to me with his apple red cheeks.
To convince folks of this would surely take weeks.
He said hop in my sleigh, and we'll ride out of here.
Just leave it to me and my trusty reindeer.

I hopped in his sleigh and off we went.
I kept telling Santa he was heaven sent.
He dropped me off at my family's place.
Happiness was written all over my face.

I said thank you Santa for such great service.

He said no problem; sir you certainly deserve this.

I told Santa Claus he was welcomed to stop in.

He told me he couldn't because he had to go shoppin.'

I said, "Santa Claus do you really go shopping?"

He said, "Sure and this year's list is really popping!"

I said, "Your service to the communities is always good."

"By the way, please make it back to my neighborhood."

He said, "Here's something for you and your folks to hear."

"Merry Christmas and a happy new year!"

I petted his reindeer, and they licked my face.

I was feeling weird and sort of out of place.

I woke up from what was apparently a dream.

I was still at my house, you see what I mean?

My dog was the one licking my face.

He was covering me with drool at a rapid pace.

If this were true, it would be hard to believe.

But it still turned out to be "A memorable Christmas Eve."

TALKING ABOUT THE "N" WORD

You use the "N" word like it's going out of style.
It's not just insulting but it's also vile.
A six-letter word with so many implications.
A word that has caused marches and demonstrations.

You use the word as if it's a term of endearment.
Why is your use of the "N" word so frequent?
Do you even know the meaning of the word?
Calling each other that is extremely absurd.

If a white person said it you'd be ready to fight.
But as long as it's your own folks it's cool and all right.
I hear the word so often I can't even stand it.
I wouldn't feel bad if our Lawmakers banned it!

Rapper does that word help your rhymes flow?

Are there any more positive words that you know?

Does saying the “N” word empower you?

Can you go without using it an hour or two?

Whoops you slipped up and said it again!

Do all of your sentences have to start with “N?”

Are you trying to show your level of intelligence?

You use it every sentence, but you never make sense!

You say, “I use the “N” word, but I don’t really curse.”

But by using that word you have done even worse.

It was the first word your child ever said.

He knew that word before he ever read.

I ask what kind of example you are setting.

Certainly not a good one is what I’m betting.

Take the “N” word out of your vocabulary.

The inability to express yourself is only momentary.

It's the most degrading word our race has heard.

Please don't continue to use the "N" word!

THOUGHTS OF YOU

It's not just today that you're on my mind.
It's every day and all the time.
From when I awaken until I go to bed.
You're in my thoughts and in my head.

I wonder what you've done to me.
These feelings are strong can't you see?
I long to see you and hold you tight.
Just feeling your warmth would be all right.

A box of candy or a long-stemmed rose.
I'd rather kiss you from your head to your toes.
Just wanting to wake up next to you.
Thinking of all the naughty things we'd do.

Wanting to kiss those beautiful lips.
And wrap my arms around those sexy hips.
I'm just letting you know how I feel.
There's no mistaking that I'm for real.

No matter what you do from day to day.
I'll be in your thoughts I hope and pray.
No distance can keep us apart.
You'll stay in my mind, and you'll stay in my heart.

I'm sure you'll say as you read this poem.
"He's unpredictable but I'm sure I know him."
You'll say, "He not always easy for me to understand."
"But I'm proud to say that he's my man!"

WHEN WE FIRST MET

I think about when we first met.
It's etched in your mind as well I bet.
Checking out your sexy smile.
It was on my mind for quite a while.

You said hello with uncertainty.
Could you be an Angel who was sent here to me?
I couldn't talk and was somewhat speechless.
I was quite unprepared I have to confess.

I felt really nervous and completely out of place.
I'm sure it was written all over my face.
I thought that maybe I should remain quiet.
I was acting shy, but you wouldn't buy it.

You turned and smiled as you walked away.
I thought about you for the rest of the day.

I wondered if we would meet again.
I believed we would but wondered when.
I met you again at the very same spot.
You were dressed quite sexy and were looking really hot.

This time I spoke to you with lots of confidence.
I knew you wouldn't go for that silent nonsense.
I was hoping to at least get your phone number.
If I couldn't do that it would be such a bummer!

We sat at a table and conversed for a while.
I can honestly say I liked your style.
We decided to set up another date.
I thought you might just be my soul mate.

We have been a couple for a very long time.
I will ask for your hand so that you can be mine.
We have had sometimes that I won't forget.
And I still daydream about "When we first met."

WITHOUT A VOICE: THE NON-VOTER

"I don't believe it matters if I vote."
Those are your exact words and that's an exact quote.
Many have died for you to have that right.
Their diligence and sacrifices helped win the fight.

If you don't vote, how can you complain?
You vent about the system but it's all in vain.
You say, "They don't really care about us!"
Electing someone who does is what we need to discuss.

What if half our voices were never heard?
It would be just as sad if it were only one third.
You say that you don't like the candidate.
But by not voting you have sealed your own fate.

It's not whether the candidate has your approval.
If they ignore the issues voting can force their removal.
Homelessness, hopelessness and so much despair.
We all can agree that the system's unfair.

Our situation isn't going to change over night.
But your voice must be heard so exercise your right!
It's called a right but it's more like an obligation.
How else will they hear about all your frustration?

By simply voting we can empower our community.
There is strength in numbers so there has to be unity.
"Keep hope alive," says Reverend Jesse Jackson.
Our fight is not over it has only just begun.

Voting helps us to keep hope alive.
All we want is for our families to thrive.
If you don't vote you are "Without a voice,"
Become a voter there is no other choice!

YOU CALL HER A BITCH AND A HO

A Bitch is a female dog, and a Ho does it for money.
Yet these are names that you're calling your honey.
Why do you treat her with such disrespect?
On these words of wisdom, you need to reflect.

Ladies those names are definitely not cute.
He doesn't respect you so give him the boot!
Rapper those names are degrading and offensive.
Can you show your talent and be more creative?

You degrade our sisters when all else fails.
Is that the only way for you to boost record sales?
When a white person calls her that, we march and protest.
Until they are punished, we do not rest!

You said, "In this industry it's what sells best."

It's not just you but your label we contest!

I do not believe in double standards.

I get upset no matter who says those words!

I am not saying the answer is censorship.

But some way some how we need to get a grip!

We want respect but we don't respect ourselves.

Let's keep offensive music off the store shelves!

I have one more thing that I need to let you know.

She is a beautiful woman, not a "Bitch or a Ho!"

EDUCATED BUT DEADLY: A SCHOOL-SHOOTING SUSPECT

You have done everything in your power just to be accepted.
Nobody ever listens to you, and you feel quite rejected.
No matter how hard you try, you just don't fit in.
Your list of friends and associates has gotten real thin.

Your peers now tease you on a regular basis.
It seems to be happening in more and more places.
You reach out for help but nobody pays attention.
You're becoming disruptive and you stay in detention.

Your parents keep saying it's just growing pains.
Yet the emptiness you feel always remains.
They feel you have everything you could possibly need.
You're a walking time bomb and they better take heed!

You're having thoughts of committing suicide.
You wonder who would care if you just up and died.

Your frustration has turned into anger and hate.
Your grades are dropping at an alarming rate.
You want to do something to get some attention.
Last week your behavior caused your suspension.

You're heading down a dangerous and destructive path.
You want everyone in the school to feel your wrath.
Everyone, including your family, has given up on you.
They have no idea of what you're planning to do.

You buy a gun that can kill lots of people.
It holds plenty of bullets and it's sure to be lethal.
As you stuff the weapon in your faded blue jeans.
You start thinking about what all of this means.

You decide to give what you're plotting some thought.
It means hard time or death if you were to be caught.
You are very angry but you're too young to die.
You decide it's time to give God a try.

You look towards the sky for divine intervention.

You say a long prayer to get God's attention.

Your life has begun to change for the better.

Your school just gave you a commendation letter.

You have accepted the fact that you are simply different.

Your time with God was time well spent.

You started to gain confidence and more self-respect.

Thank God you didn't become a "School shooting suspect!"

DANGEROUS AND ARMED: GUN-OWNERS

It's starting to get like the wild wild west.
Will you have to put your gun-slinging skills to the test?
Gone are the days of the old six-shooter.
Now you can buy an assault rifle from your computer.

You think you are safer if you possess a gun.
Who really wins when all is said and done?
You're more likely to become a shooting victim yourself.
You should have left your weapon on the store shelf!

Yesterday a little boy found his father's gun.
You can imagine what happened to that father's son.
Sure, we all have the right to bear arms.
Guess how many people that right harms!

One of your guns can hold down an Army.
Bullets have no names and that's what you fail to see!
Do you listen to the garbage from the NRA?
Perhaps you're a hunter that needs an AK!

"Guns don't kill people, people do."
But what if the shooting victim happens to be you?
"Pry your gun from your cold dead hand?"
It happens quite often so please understand!

You were driving around with a gun in your car.
Someone cut you off and you went too far.
Now you are in prison doing hard time.
We both know it was a senseless crime!

Gun violence is at an all-time high.
It's scary out there I am not going to lie.
When you carry a gun, you feel safe and protected.
If you have to shoot someone, you will forever be affected.

By these words of wisdom, do not be alarmed.

But there are consequences for being "Dangerous and armed!"

KATRINA'S VICTIM AMERICA'S VICTIM

"Evacuate New Orleans because Katrina is upon us!"
Your poor evacuation plan is what we need to discuss!
Many of us simply did not have transportation.
That should have been taken into consideration.

Several of my relatives perished in the storm.
You treated my family as if this was the norm.
Why did it take you so long to arrive?
It is a miracle that many of us were able to survive!

You had plenty of warning about this disaster.
Your response should have been considerably faster!
You needed a reason for taking your time.
You blamed it on the looting, shooting and crime.

There is much to be learned about your rescue efforts.

They were quite disorganized you can just ask the experts.

Perhaps there were plenty of lessons to be learned.

The bad publicity you received was definitely well earned.

We appreciate our soldiers, rescuers and heroes.

They bravely risked their lives, which everyone knows.

What did the finger pointing really achieve?

We still do not know whom we should believe!

I do not believe the response was a racial issue.

But for your incompetence we should surely dismiss you.

We are American citizens we are not the enemy.

We are from a country known as, "Land of the free."

Most of us already lived check-to-check.

To make things worse now our homes are a wreck.

My family and I have lost everything we own.

We have each other but we still feel alone.

There is lots of red tape and nobody wants to help us.

That is the main reason we feel such disgust!

I am hoping to return to New Orleans some day.

She will bounce back from this we all hope and pray.

People ask themselves, "Why did this happen to them?"

We simply became "Katrina's Victim" then "America's Victim."

THE WAR ON TERROR:

CAN WE WIN?

Where are the weapons of mass destruction?
You bombed Iraq until it needs reconstruction.
You removed the evil Dictator Saddam Hussein.
You were instrumental in ending his terrible reign.

Many Soldiers died in this so-called war on terror.
We thought the conditions there would get much better.
Removing a Dictator does not mean peace.
This has been proven in the Middle East.

You said, "This is a war that will be won!"
At what cost to us when it's over and done?
We are all asking, "Exactly who is the enemy?"
At this point there is no telling who it might be.

It is a country filled with fighting and pandemonium.
You claim things are better, but we are not dumb!
Soldiers are dying daily from terrorist acts.
I am telling the truth and those are the facts!

Why are you refusing to give a timetable?
Perhaps we should leave while we are still able.
We love and support our Troops and Soldiers.
They are doing their job and following orders.

They knew the risks when they joined the Service.
But we are still wondering if they really deserve this.
We hope their sacrifices are not in vain.
All the casualties have caused an emotional drain.

We hope and pray that the peace will begin.
As for the war on terror, "Can we really win?"

A SECOND EDITION

I have decided to do a second edition.
It was a no brainer, an easy decision.
I developed a bad case of Writer's block.
I started to believe I was against the clock.

Will it be as passionate as my first book?
I remembered the sacrifices that edition took.
After all, I always strive for perfection.
I had to learn to deal with rejection.

I tried to think of some encouraging words.
A blinking curser is for the birds!
For hours I stared at a blank page.
I started believing I was beginning to age.

Should I stay with the same genre and flow?

There are still quite a few social issues to go.

I am determined to make an impact on society.

Perhaps I should have taken up psychiatry.

Inspiring and educating is my primary mission.

Therefore, I am doing "A Second edition."

INDECENT EXPOSURE

Why do you dress like a Prostitute on duty?
Your skirt is so high you are showing your booty.
Your shirt is wide open, and your breasts are showing.
Are you starting to see where this poem is going?

You were barely able to squeeze in that dress.
You're showing all your goods and looking a mess!
Your designer jeans look painted on.
Is your self-respect totally gone?

Perhaps your problem is low self-esteem.
You want some attention, and you know what I mean.
I am sure you receive a lot of attention.
Guys want to do things to you I can't even mention.

Most of them don't even care to know you.

They just want to have fun and do what they do!

To them you just appear to be easy.

Folks around town say you dress really sleazy.

You're a beautiful young lady but you dress like a whore.

You seem to be wearing less and less more and more.

You hear me but do you really understand me?

I am not saying you have to dress like a granny!

Just dress like a respectable young lady.

The way you dress right now is definitely crazy!

To write this poem I had to maintain my composure.

But I just had to address your "Indecent Exposure."

TRASH MOUTH

Can you express yourself without the use of profanity?
Cursing the way you do is pure insanity!
It only shows a lack of intelligence.
Hence, it reveals one's stupidity and ignorance.

Please watch that profanity young lady.
You curse like a Sailor on a ship in the Navy!
You even curse around your children at times.
They recite profanity not nursery rhymes!

Do you think it's cute to hear them curse?
Their profanity will only get worse.
Rapper your lyrics are not comprehensive.
You curse too much and you're way too offensive.

You have already made millions doing it the wrong way.

Perhaps you will become part of the solution someday.

It appears you have a limited vocabulary.

I suggest you get educated and invest in a dictionary.

Where you're from cursing makes you a cool cat.

But it's not where you're from it's where you're at.

Whether you're from the East, West, North or South.

Try expressing yourself without being a "Trash mouth!"

BLACK ON BLACK:
CRIME IN THE HOOD

Why do we continue to wipe each other out?
Your ability to survive the hood is already in doubt.
Statistics say you will eventually become a victim.
You're black in the hood and your future looks grim.

You cannot continue to blame "the man."
You need to be proactive and have yourself a plan.
Take responsibility for your actions and decisions.
I may just reiterate this in future editions.

Yes, our young folks are killing each other.
But should we blame a teacher, father or mother?
You robbed someone who has less than you do.
You blasted that young man with a stolen twenty-two.

You took his life for a meager ten bucks.

Now you're incarcerated and that really sucks!

You're so young and had your whole life ahead of you.

You could have beat the odds like a chosen few.

Now you are part of a dismal statistic.

Young, black and in prison to be more specific.

You're more likely to go to prison than to college.

You need to start believing in the power of knowledge.

You witness criminal activity and turn the other way.

Word on the street is, "You snitch and you pay!"

Do you feel it is necessary to live in fear?

Am I telling you things you don't want to hear?

How long will you stand by and do nothing?

What do you think your silence will bring?

You cannot escape crime by locking your door.

Things are happening around you that you shouldn't ignore.

The crime in your neighborhood never stops.
Another problem is you don't trust the cops.
It has to be a community and police effort.
Just give it a try, I am sure it can't hurt.

If you want change, you have to do something different.
Your time making a difference will be time well spent.
So be sure to get involved in your community.
It's the only way there will ever be unity.

These views and opinions are strictly mine.
I hope you agree with me but if you don't that's fine.
I wrote these words to give something back.
I hope they're instrumental in stopping the "Black on black."

GHETTO MENTALLITY:
CAPTIVITY OF THE MIND

You moved from the ghetto, but have you really gone?
It's still a part of you and you just can't move on.
You're out of the ghetto but it's not out of you.
You're extremely confused and don't know what to do.

You've moved on up, but you really don't fit in.
You want to start over but don't know how to begin.
This neighborhood is cleaner and a whole lot safer.
Your chances to thrive are a whole lot greater.

People in the neighborhood look at you crazy.
You said, "They don't know me so that doesn't phase me."
You cruise through the block with your radio bumping.
You party all night and have your whole house jumping.

You invite friends and folks from the old neighborhood.
Some of those characters were up to no good!
That's why your neighbors didn't want you there.
You swore up and down they were being unfair.

Crime is on the rise in their once peaceful community.
Back in your old hood is where they want you to be.
You never knew how good you had it.
Your ghetto-like behavior was a force of habit.

Property values go down and people move out.
It's the demise of the neighborhood without a doubt.
Now you have successfully brought the ghetto there.
Sad thing about it is that you don't even care.

You don't see the big picture, perhaps you're blind.
You suffer from a bad case of "Captivity of the mind."

WITHOUT JUSTICE WITHOUT PEACE:

UNEQUAL JUSTICE IN AMERICA

When will there be equal justice in America?
Our current system is causing mass hysteria!
White justice, black justice, rich justice, poor justice.
An even playing field seems almost hopeless.

How can you find an unbiased jury?
The unfair system is what fuels our fury.
If you are rich, you can afford a dream team.
You can get away with murder or so it would seem.

If you're poor or black, it's harder to prove your innocence.
It is imperative that you have a strong defense.
Do you believe that every black man is a criminal?
Are the negative messages about us strictly subliminal?

I have never committed or been convicted of a crime.
But if I am accused of one I am more likely to do time.
You said he would have a jury of his peers.
But it was an all-white jury with stereotypes and fears.

Supposedly, America has the best judicial system.
But sometimes it seems like it's us against them.
You locked that young man up for twenty-two years.
So many years of blood, sweat and tears.

DNA proved that the young man was innocent.
Those who took his freedom should surely repent.
The all-white jury never evaluated the facts.
They already had preconceived notions about blacks.

You pulled that black man over in his upscale neighborhood.
You couldn't believe an honest black man could be living that good.
You shot that man forty times and took his life.
You claim you thought that he had a gun or a knife.

You killed an elderly black woman on a “no-knock” warrant.
We knew why it happened, and we understood what it meant.
You beat up a suspect and the whole incident was taped.
But from criminal charges you almost escaped.

A judge and jury cleared you of all charges.
You were only retried because of protests and marches.
You charged them with attempted murder for a schoolyard fight.
Would the charge be the same if they were all white?

Our justice system is what makes America great.
But it’s an unfair system that we have all come to hate.
Just like the sixties we have to march and protest.
Until there is equal justice we cannot rest.

May this poem reach New York to Cali and all states between.
And a copy to the Justice Department so they know what we mean.
We hope the injustices in our system will someday cease.
For if we are “Without justice” we are “Without peace.”

THE JUICED ATHLETE:

STEROID USE IN SPORTS

You hit that ball out of the park more than any other man.

But you shattered the record with a deceptive plan.

You were the strongest and fastest woman on the track.

But you had to give all of your gold medals back.

You outboxed some of the best fighters in the ring.

From your powerful hook they felt the sting.

You lifted more than any bodybuilder did in your weight class.

You had freakish strength and lots of muscle mass.

You are a massive wrestler, who is feared and respected.

You took designer drugs that were never detected.

It is okay to be passionate about reaching your goal.

But it does not mean you have to sell your soul!

What kind of example are you setting for our youth?

Would they still look up to you if they knew the truth?

After all is said and done your nothing but a cheater.

If it had been an honest victory, it would be much sweeter.

You refused to experience the agony of defeat.

In your quest for victory, you became a "Juiced athlete."

MARCHING TO A DIFFERENT BEAT

Today we march to a different beat.

We embrace victory but we reject defeat.

We accomplish this through hard work and dedication.

We are dedicated to this but first comes education.

We are dedicated to preserving our school's tradition.

In fact, that happens to be our most important mission!

So, as we march on this unforgiving field.

We know what the fruits of our labor will yield.

When we march, we put our best foot forward.

With these powerful words, our voices will be heard.

We recite this poem loudly so our competitors can hear it.

May they witness on this day our undying spirit.

Whether the scoreboard says it is a loss or win.

We gave our best effort and showed pride from within.

We will be diligent in accomplishing our missions and goals.

You can feel the power from our mighty marching souls!

Our competitors will simply have to take a back seat.

For today we are all, "Marching to a different beat."

THE CALL TO DUTY:
A SOLDIER'S POEM

I went straight from High school into the service.
I was feeling proud but extremely nervous.
My mother cried with tears of joy.
She said, "I will try to stop referring to you as my little boy."

I arrived at Basic Training with a busload of candidates.
We were greeted quite loudly at the main entry gates.
The Drill Sergeants called us everything they could think of.
We knew, at least from them, we would receive no love.

We were too young to drink and barely able to vote.
We were all different races, but we were in the same boat.
We had eight weeks to learn how to work as a team.
We started to believe that it was all a bad dream!

We went to bed late but were up before dawn.
We do more before nine is definitely right on!
Basic Training was tough, but we all got through it.
Things would get worst, and we pretty much knew it.

We would be on the front lines as Infantry Soldiers.
There would be a lot of responsibility put on our shoulders.
The first orders we received took us to the Middle East.
Our primary mission was to bring about peace.

For the first time in our lives, we were in a foreign land.
The things we saw you could never understand.
The precision bombings caused so much destruction.
The whole place looks like it needs reconstruction.

We are under attack on a regular basis.
Our so-called enemy is in more and more places.
Perhaps we are acquiring more and more enemies.
The hate for us here is like an infectious disease.

We were instrumental in removing a terrible dictator.
But the level of danger here has gotten even greater.
Nobody wants to admit that we are in a civil war.
Many of us are now on our second or third tour.

I have lost some of my comrades along the way.
We all know the risks and that is all I can say.
We will defend our country from all enemies, foreign and domestic.
We are a force to be reckoned with, and we are not to be messed with!

We will win this so-called war on terror.
Messing with the United States was their biggest error!
A successful completion of our mission would be a thing of beauty.
We are proud we answered, "The call to duty."

A LONG KISS GOODBYE

To me, she is like a rare diamond or pearl.

I am so proud to say that she is my girl.

Last night I found it difficult to sleep.

My thoughts about her were oh so deep.

I held her tightly for most of the night.

I wouldn't even turn off the bedroom light.

I laid there watching her as she slept.

She was looking quite beautiful and so well kept.

As I lay there, tears began to roll down my cheeks.

I would be leaving her for approximately eight weeks.

I would be leaving her for another short tour.

Uncle Sam keeps us apart more and more.

Don't get me wrong I do love the service.
I am serving my country as an Army Reservist.
The morning arrived quicker than I anticipated.
When I am with her, sleep seems so overrated.

We miss each other so much when I am gone.
It seems each day apart goes on and on.
It all began to sink in as I started getting dressed.
The thought of us being apart was making me stressed.

She woke up and stretched her arms out to me.
I went back in her arms where she needed me to be.
She let me know that she would always love me.
And when we're apart she always thinks of me.

I held her tightly and she began to cry.
I proceeded to give her "A long kiss goodbye."

HOMELESS

As a teenager, I was the recipient of a lot of misfortune.
I went through so much and often took it on the chin.
We all know when it rains it pours.
I saw few opportunities and many closed doors.

I made my bed hard, and I had to lay in it.
I made poor decisions, and I am not just sayin' it.
I was hardheaded as hell and a high school dropout.
My future looked grim and certainly in doubt.

My mother said I had to go to work or to school.
Just laying around the house was no longer cool.
I was getting into trouble and just being bad.
I blamed it on the fact that I didn't have a dad.

She kicked me out while I was still just a teen.
At the time, I didn't realize what it would all mean.
Without an education, I could not find work.
I was pulling out my hair and going berserk.

I wondered the streets daily like a poor lost child.
In the streets at such a young age was extremely wild.
Sometimes my meal came from a garbage can.
I felt more like an animal and less like a man.

Sometimes it was difficult to find a warm meal.
There were times when I felt it was easier to steal.
I spent many nights sleeping outside in the elements.
I knew getting out of this would take lots of diligence.

I did things to make money, none that I am proud of.
I prayed for divine intervention from the Lord above.
I said, "Lord let me survive this a little while longer."
I knew if it didn't kill me, it would make me much stronger.

I had to gain confidence in my ability to survive.
I knew I could come out of this, and I knew I could thrive.
I began to wonder to what else I would be subjected.
Help came to me much quicker than expected.

I joined a program to help me get my education.
I had to try my best was the only stipulation.
I did my best and I managed to graduate.
I was doing something positive and feeling very great.

My mother made sure she attended my graduation.
She smiled at me proudly but there was no celebration.
She always knew I was an intelligent young man.
Her scared straight tactic was a masterful plan.

She never doubted that I would survive.
She had faith that the Lord would keep me alive.
She was doing what she felt needed to be done.
She said, "It was the only way for me to wake you up son!"

Now I have a job, my own place and money in the bank.

I have the Lord, my mother and myself to thank.

My life could have ended up a very tragic story.

I praise God daily and give him the glory.

I give back to my community; I have become quite generous.

I am a better man because I overcame being "Homeless."

"YES, I CAN HEAR YOU NOW!"

Many of us wonder if cell phones were a good invention.
They distract so many of us and take so much of our attention.
Do you think everyone wants to hear your conversation?
You are the loudest person in the entire nation!

I can hear your conversation clear across the room.
It sounds like your life is full of drama and gloom.
You're doing twenty in a sixty-five mile an hour zone.
I pass you cautiously because you are on your cell phone.

You are holding up traffic and driving erratic.
Shut up and drive or the results will be tragic!
Driving while talking is like driving while intoxicated.
They both cause accidents the driver never anticipated.

You are on your phone everywhere, including the bank.

For your annoying conversation we have technology to thank.

Wait for an appropriate time to talk on your phone.

Once upon a time we waited until we got home.

Perhaps, like cigarettes they should have a warning label.

When purchased, their dangers should be discussed at the table.

Lawmakers are making changes and should take a bow.

To emphatically answer your question, "Yes I can hear you now!"

I CRY YET I LAUGH:
I AM SAD YET I AM HAPPY

Few people have seen me cry.
On occasions, many have seen me sigh.
I cried yet you never saw my tears.
I hid my emotions along with my fears.

You were able to see through all of my laughter.
You knew it was only true happiness I was after.
It was so easy for me to open up to you.
When times were hard and my friends were few.

You were the one person I could always depend on.
You were there for me when everyone else was gone.
Even when I am sad, few people know it.
I smile a lot and try not to show it.

You accepted me, for who I was.

You ignored all the rumors and negative buzz.

You were always such a good friend to me.

Nothing will change and you will always be.

Now I will be smiling towards the heavens above.

You will still be the friend I always think of.

It seems I have so many emotions coming at me.

But still, “I cry yet I laugh” and “I am sad yet I am happy.”

EDUCATING THE VILLAGE:
AN EDUCATOR'S POEM

You spend countless hours educating our youth.
"It takes a village to raise them" is certainly the truth.
They are our future and education is the key.
You are helping them be all that they can be.

Your resources are limited but you get the job done.
You have the tough job of keeping learning fun.
"Leave no child behind," was your intended mission.
But if they don't make the grade, you have a tough decision.

You are constantly preparing and reviewing lesson plans.
You continually make sure every child understands.
You're always grading test papers, homework and schoolwork.
Mercifully, the school year ends before you go berserk.

Sometimes you have students that are not so cooperative.

We often wonder when your patience will give.

You follow your game plan for each child, year after year.

You face these great challenges with very little fear.

Please know that your sacrifices are not in vain.

There will be some days of sunshine and some days of rain.

They will continue to learn if you continue to show them.

I am hoping to inspire you with "An Educator's poem."

"I AM HERE FOR YOU NOW SON:"

A POEM FOR MY SON BRAD

I missed so many years and so many birthdays.

I missed seeing you grow up in so many ways.

I never got to wonder if you were a boy or a girl.

I never even witnessed you enter this world.

I never got a chance to hear you say daddy.

I never disciplined you when you were behaving badly.

I never held you when you began to cry.

It hurts quite a bit I am not going to lie.

I missed your transition from childhood to manhood.

But fortunately, you still were able to turn out good.

Your mother raised you to be a fine young man.

She did a good job and stuck to her plan.

I simply never knew that you were my child.

Finding out so abruptly was extremely wild.

The years we lost together are now behind us.

We have so much to catch up on and so much to discuss.

Words can never express how I feel.

I pinched myself to make sure it's all real.

My relationship with you as your father has only just begun.

And I just needed you to know, "I am here for you now son."

FATHERLESS:

A SINGLE MOTHERS' POEM

He promised you the world and everything in it.
You never doubted him, not even for a minute.
You thought he would be there for you and the baby.
Will he ever be in the child's life? You still say, "Maybe."

He manipulated you and played with your mind.
He chose to leave you and the baby behind.
You loved your husband unconditionally, with all your heart.
However, irreconcilable differences broke you two apart.

It was a tough custody battle but you got the children.
He promised to help out but you often wondered when.
You consistently pursue him for financial support.
You have spent countless hours in Family Court.

You know financial support is simply not enough.
Raising a child without a father is extremely tough.
You're turning boys into men and girls into ladies.
They certainly don't stay cute little babies!

You have had sleepless nights and endless days.
Why should you be the only one who pays?
So many children growing up without a father.
I could quote statistics but why even bother?

We know it is a serious problem with serious consequences.
The mother and child suffer in so many instances.
You begin to feel like you are on your own.
But the Lord is with you so you are not alone.

Just continue to try hard and do your best.
The Lord above will take care of the rest.
Be the best single parent that you can be.
You will certainly be blessed, just wait and see.

No more tears for you are a strong young lady.

Do not let single parenthood drive you crazy.

Every day of your life is now a Mother's Day.

I hope I have inspired you in a very special way.

It will be okay if your children never know him.

Please hear these words from, "A single mothers' poem."

"LISTEN AND BE QUIET!"

Please be quiet sometimes and just simply listen.
Perhaps you will find out what you have been missin.'
The **"L"** in listen stands for **LEARN**.
You have done your talking so now it's my turn.

The **"I"** in listen stands for **INTERESTING**.
Being a good listener is sometimes the best thing.
The **"S"** in listen stands for **SUBJECTS**.
You know it all, you're one of the usual suspects!

The **"T"** in listen stands for **THROUGH**.
Just two more letters, I'll be finished in a few.
The **"E"** in listen stands for **EDUCATION**.
Getting to the top takes hard work and dedication.

The **"N"** in listen stands for **NOW**.

I've educated you on the word listen and have taken a bow.

You still keep on talking and refuse to try it.

Do yourself a favor, just "Listen and be quiet!"

L.I.S.T.E.N

"**L**earn **I**nteresting **S**ubjects **T**hrough **E**ducation **N**ow!"

THE STATE OF THE HOOD:
EMPOWERMENT BY INVOLVEMENT

More and more people are choosing to get involved.
However, there are still problems that need to be resolved.
Many of us know what needs to be done.
We have chosen to fight and will no longer run.

You now know that you can make a difference.
You have mentored some of our at-risk youth for instance.
You let them know there are no excuses to fail.
And that life is not a joke nor a huge fairy tale.

Continue strengthening our families and our communities will follow.
Perhaps there are a few of Bill Cosby's lines to borrow.
Fathers are starting to play a role in raising their children.
You're there for them now so she doesn't care where you've been.

Sometimes we put ourselves in terrible positions.
We don't always think before we make our decisions.
If you make your bed hard, you will surely have to lay in it.
After all is said and done, it is your life you're playin' with.

Even though you may have more than one problem.
You know having a plan is the only way to solve them.
What are you doing to improve your situation?
No excuses or complaining is my only stipulation.

Nothing gets done by making excuses and complaining.
Even if you make excuses until there are no more remaining.
We have stopped turning our heads and slamming our door.
Now criminals are the ones becoming victims more and more.

Our young folks are learning that education is the key.
They have opened their eyes and can finally see.
They know they are in control of their own future.
And there is a whole world outside their television and computer.

You don't have to become a product of your environment.
I have said it before, now you understand what I meant.
You are finally realizing there are no shortcuts to success.
The only shortcuts I know cause heartache and stress.

Our neighborhoods are getting better and that is certainly good.
This is just my observation about, "The state of the hood."
I will close this poem with a very important comment.
Unity in the community equals, "Empowerment by involvement."

THE STATE OF OUR NATION

Can any candidate fix the mess we are in?
The main question should be, "How should they begin?"
For the first time, a black candidate and female candidate are running.
If either becomes president, it will be both amazing and stunning.

We are feeling the pinch from the weakness of the dollar.
The prices are so high it makes us want to holler!
We have waged a seemingly endless war on terror.
Hindsight is twenty-twenty but was it a huge error?

So many homes have gone into foreclosure.
Families are finding it hard to keep their composure.
You balanced the budget but at what cost?
Just look at how many jobs have already been lost!

Many of us have several jobs to make ends meet.
But we are still one bill away from being in the street!
There is constant blaming and bipartisan bickering.
But behind closed doors, perhaps they're all snickering.

No matter who takes the helm their task will be great.
We will choose a candidate, and we will choose our fate.
America will bounce back as she always does.
We will all be saying, "I remember how it once was."

All we have to do is weather the storm.
Sadly, for now, struggling will be the norm.
Right now, there is a lot of fear, anger and frustration.
Unfortunately, that is the current, "State of our nation."

A TOUGH LIFE: A PERSONAL BIOGRAPHY

I was born on March 9, 1965, in a city that does not sleep.
A city where the winters are so cold they make you want to weep!
Yes, I am talking about New York City.
I am going to tell my story, but I do not expect pity.

Both parents abandoned me at the tender age of four.
Statistically, I was destined to fail right out the door.
Put in foster care with my three sisters and two brothers.
Thank God, I was able to stay with the others!

Growing up, I had four sets of foster parents all together.
Yeah, I know, one good set would have surely been better.
Most of them treated us fairly well.
However, the first set put us through quite a bit of hell.

Yes, there was verbal and physical abuse.

On many occasions, I went to bed hungry with a whelp or bruise.

There is a difference between a spanking and a beating.

I know because I have been beat with just about everything!

In most cases, the verbal and physical abuse tends to scar.

However, it can also shape you as a person and determine who you are.

I could have ended up in a lifetime of crime.

I could have ended up incarcerated, still doing hard time.

I could have been addicted to drugs or alcohol.

However, I had big dreams and needed to stand tall.

I had plenty of opportunities to join a gang.

I just never had the heart to be a thug or to bang.

I could very well have ended up dead.

I had too much to accomplish and big dreams of getting ahead.

I graduated from high school, class of '83.

I felt extremely proud and somewhat free.

I decided to join the United States Navy.
I enjoyed it, but being at sea so much can be a little crazy.
I sailed all over and visited many different places.
I saw many different cultures and many different faces.

I was honorably discharged from the Navy in 1986.
Now a civilian, I had to get right back into the mix.
I felt a little more time in the service would not harm me.
After a few short months, I joined the United States Army.

I was honorably discharged from the Army in 1992.
Once again, a free man, but still unsure about what I wanted to do.
I did many different jobs just to pay the bills and eat.
It was extremely tough to make ends meet.

I even remember sleeping in my ride.
Failure was not an option because I have too much pride.
I was now a resident of the very expensive, "Golden state."
Where there are beautiful beaches and the weather is great.

I discovered my writing talent in 1993, while being a Security Guard.

At first, it became an escape for me when times got hard.

I later decided to utilize this skill to educate our communities.

Getting others involved in this effort was certainly no breeze!

From 1995 to 2000, I wrote, directed and acted in four educational plays.

I was saving lives and getting folks to change their ways.

I have since written several screenplays and educational books of poetry.

With my poetry, you can just listen to my messages or feel free to flow with me.

In 2004, I came to the "Peach State," otherwise known as, "The A-T-L."

To get there, I drove coast-to-coast, which was sort of like hell.

I continued to write as well as keep a nine-to-five.

It was the only way for me to thrive.

I began to volunteer in schools as a Youth Motivational Speaker.
Doing that kind of work actually made me meeker.
In 2008 I found out I have a son.
He stays here in Atlanta, and he is now twenty-one.

He was conceived while I was stationed in Atlanta in the Army.
When I found out, I was so excited it took several weeks to calm me.
Suddenly, I had to take on the role of fatherhood.
We have developed a relationship and so far, everything is good.

My second edition poetry book is dedicated to my son Brad.
I have this feeling that he is proud of his dad.
Unfortunately, I have never been able to find my parents.
There has never been closure, so it has never made sense.

I stay in touch with my brothers and sisters as much as I can.
We will continue to seek closure at least that is the plan.
I also stay in touch with my last two sets of foster parents.
Occasionally, I will just surprise them with a phone call for instance.

Writing, motivating and educating others was certainly a good decision.
Many years ago, it became my primary mission.
I really just love to write; I am not going to lie.
Just bury me with a pen and pad whenever I die!

I am now CEO and Founder of Tavares Entertainment, LLC.
I offer creative writing services and speaking for a small fee.
I will continue to do what I do best.
Until I leave an indelible mark on society, I will not rest.

My life has been challenging but I am strong as you can see.
In fact, I had, "A tough life" and this is, "A personal biography."

AN ATMOSPHERE OF HATRED

When will there be equality for all mankind?

In the twenty-first century, in America, it is still impossible to find.

Without it, America will never be a great nation.

The hatred and racism go from generation to generation.

However, it is true that all men are created equal.

I will reiterate this point and as for this poem, it may need a sequel.

Racism is caused by fear and ignorance.

Either you're a racist or you aren't, you can't sit on the fence.

You are not judging me by the content of my character.

To you, me being black is a negative factor.

There is so much more to me than meets the eye.

Can you please give acceptance and tolerance a try?

Racism is not just between blacks and whites.

Everyone in America is entitled to equal rights!

So please educate yourself about other cultures and races.

We are a nation of people from many different places.

We can accomplish so much if we just respect each other.

This should be taught by every father and mother.

If we cannot accept each other problems are created.

It can only lead to, "An atmosphere of hatred."

"TO MY SON WITH LOVE"

When you were born, I remember looking into your eyes.
How much of a blessing you are is what I began to realize.
Before you were born, I had so many challenges coming at me.
Yet after you were born, you made me feel so happy.

You made my days look a whole lot brighter.
I knew I needed to be a strong mother and somewhat of a fighter.
I know things will not always be easy for us.
However, serving our Lord and savior will surely be a plus.

I am sharing my thoughts for you with this poetry that rhymes.
I look forward to us having a whole lot of good times.
I look forward to hearing your words the first time you talk.
I look forward to seeing you crawl, your first steps and when you finally walk.

I look forward to your first day of school.

I will make sure you know education is a powerful tool.

I look forward to all your graduations.

I will make sure to give you lots of congratulations.

I will do my part to make you a strong man.

I will teach you never to say, “I can’t” but always to say, “I can.”

I will always believe you are a blessing from above.

This poem is very sincerely, “To my son with love.”

EXPRESSIONS OF LOVE TO A WONDERFUL AUNT

For all the times you were just there.

Moreover, the many times you just showed me you care.

For all the times you believed in me.

You told me I could be whatever I want to be.

We were always very close to each other.

You were sort of like a second mother.

You have helped me to become a strong man.

I am expressing my love for you the best I can.

We have accomplished so much together.

You always managed to make things better.

You made me believe that my future was bright.

All I had to do was to do what was right.

I wanted to thank you from the bottom of my heart.

I believe this poem is certainly a good start.

Just letting you know how I feel is all I want.

These are, "Expressions of love to a wonderful Aunt."

FROM A DREAM TO REALITY:
A HISTORIC ELECTION

The two thousand eight Presidential elections will go down in history.
For many of us, it was such a huge victory.
African Americans were part of a huge voter turnout.
However, we still had some doubt.

After all, the Presidency has been stolen before.
If it happened again there would be a huge uproar!
We now know that voting can be effective.
We look at it from a completely new perspective.

The dream came true forty-five years later.
The timing for this event could not be greater.
Barack Obama was not judged by the color of his skin.
It was the content of his character and his strength from within.

I never thought this could happen in my lifetime.
Perhaps in my son's but certainly not mine.
We now have a sense of hope and pride.
For this historic moment, many have died.

We have come a long way, yet we are still not there.
Unfortunately, our country is still neither equal nor fair.
Barack Obama's message of change was easy to embrace.
He used it quite effectively in this Presidential race.

He warned us that change would not happen overnight.
It is imperative we do our part and continue the fight.
It must start in our homes and communities.
There must be more accountability and less excuses please!

His other message was, "Yes we can!"
He proceeded to convince us that he is the man.
November two thousand eight will never be forgotten.
It tells us how far we have come as well as where we have been.

"From a dream to reality," is our overall perception.

This election will forever be called, "A historic election."

MODERN DAY HEROES: DOCTORS AND NURSES

You're on the front lines as our doctors and nurses
We have faith that you will eventually reverse this
You do your job without enough protective equipment
You keep being promised you'll get a new shipment

You are mentally, emotionally and physically drained
All of your resources continue to be strained
However, you continue to attack this Covid-19
It's a horrific enemy that can't be seen

This task force needs to really understand me
You are risking the health of yourself and your family
Sadly, many of your patients are dying
You hold in your emotions, there's no time for crying

You do this daily with very little rest

I wanted to let you know you all are the best

I want you to know you are appreciated

Your love for what you do is constantly demonstrated

You save people's lives, and you don't even know them

I am thanking you all with this inspirational poem.

Where your courage comes from nobody knows

but to me you are all "modern day heroes."

MODERN DAY HEROES-THE ARMED FORCES

You have the tough task of keeping the country safe for us
I was once in the service, so it is easy for me to discuss
I spent time in the Army as well as the Navy
Will I say which is my favorite? If you ask me, maybe

You're Soldiers and Marines fighting in a foreign land
You witnessed things many of us would never understand
So many tours spent in the Middle East
Where your primary mission was to bring about peace

You are under attack on a regular basis
It seems like your enemies are in more and more places
You are on the front lines of the war on terror
Proving that messing with the United States can be a huge error

You're Sailors spending much of your enlistment at sea
Just get home safely is our only plea
You hear, "This is not a drill, General Quarters! General Quarters!"
You man your battle stations, because you're in dangerous waters

Airforce, we haven't forgotten about you
We know you are a force to be reckoned with too
You know you're appreciated, but it's nice to hear it
You are dedicated to our country and have a fighting spirit

You selflessly sacrifice your lives for your country
Just so we all can live peacefully and comfy
You were there to protect us each time a threat arose
I truly believe that you are all, "modern day heroes"

MODERN DAY HEROES - POLICE OFFICERS

You respond to the call twenty-four hours a day
You lock up criminals, showing them, crime doesn't pay
You make our communities and neighborhoods safer
Our chances to live peacefully are a whole lot greater

You risk your life by simply wearing your uniform
But risking your life daily is pretty much the norm
You seldom receive credit for your heroic acts
I am telling the truth, and I am stating the facts

Robbery, murder and an occasional chase
Those are just a few things that you must face
However, you do your job day in and day out
You are certainly making a difference without a doubt

We will never forget your sacrifices on nine-eleven

Many of your comrades are now in heaven

You will say, "I am not a hero I just do my job"

But you keep us safe from those who murder, steal and rob

We know you do a lot more than just arrest people

If I mentioned everything you do, this poem would need a sequel

You make a difference in every community

We must work together if there will ever be unity

Sometimes you may feel like you're not appreciated

In your line of work, you can often feel hated

It's a dangerous but rewarding career that you chose

You are all definitely, "Modern day heroes"

MODERN DAY HEROES – FIREFIGHTERS & PARAMEDICS

A firehouse alarm sounds, breaking the night's silence,
as for the number of casualties, you are left in suspense.
The Dispatcher says, "Apartment complex fully involved,"
the issue of being short-staffed has yet to be resolved.

First alarm out, and you're the first on the scene,
from a window above, you hear a faint woman's scream.
Without thought, you rushed into the apartment,
you successfully saved a life with little time spent!

An accident with victims, a man, and his wife,
you saved their lives with your "jaws of life."
You saved countless lives as you sprang into action
"Fireman Saves Lives" read the newspaper's caption

Now you are facing this horrible disease
There is little I can say about it to put you at ease
We all know that this is a major crisis
But you stay on the front lines as we continue to fight this

Paramedics, you are on the front lines too
You continue saving lives as you do what you do.
You have accepted the fact everyone won't survive
Your challenge now is to stay healthy and alive

Some may say it's your job to save lives
It's much more than just a job is what I realize
Your dedication to saving lives definitely shows
I will always consider you to be, "Modern day heroes"

THOUGHTS OF LOVE FOR YOU FATHER

I just have so many things I want to say to you.
First, I will thank you for all you've done and for all you do.
I know you don't want me to make your day into such a big thing.
However, you need to know about the happiness you bring.

You exemplify what a good father is all about.
You're the best father in the world, hands down no doubt!
Without hesitation, you made so many sacrifices for us.
There are far too many for me to discuss.

You inspired me to do the best that I can.
You were instrumental in helping me to become a strong man.
I remember many of the things you taught me.
Your diligence has paid off as you can clearly see.

I remember your powerful lessons every day.
You always made sure I did things the right way.
I remember all the punishments and all the discipline.
You still usually managed to encourage me with a grin.

You were there to teach me so many things.
From my birth to my first steps, to tying my own shoestrings.
You were there from my first day of preschool to my high school graduation.
You encouraged me to get a college education.

You were there to make sure I did my homework and stayed in school.
You always said, “I refuse to raise an uneducated fool!”
It meant so much just to have you there.
It showed me how much you really care.

Few words can express how I feel.

These thoughts of love are definitely real.

Please know that expressing these feelings was no bother.

They are very sincerely, "Thoughts of love for you father."

THOUGHTS OF MICHAEL JACKSON:
A MUSICAL ICON AND LEGEND

We have so many things we need to say.
First, we will acknowledge that this is a very sad day.
You just always seemed to be so alive.
Many of us have watched you since the Jackson 5.

Losing you so abruptly cuts like a knife.
However, we will continue to celebrate your colorful life.
You accomplished so much in the music industry.
You always were just so amazing to see.

You have so many great albums we could discuss and review.
However, we will keep this brief and only discuss a few.
We all love your "Thriller" soundtrack.
The video made us take a breath and take a step back.

Another one of our favorites is, "Off the Wall."
The music and lyrics make us want to dance and have a ball.
The last, but certainly not least, favorite we will mention is "Bad."
There were many good songs that album had.

Your music reached many cultures and people from many countries.
You did your thing with the greatest of ease!
Even though you weren't always understood.
We can all agree that your music is good.

You were our most talented brother.
Your music made people come together and embrace each other.
Your lyrics are universal.
In my opinion, they are strong and positive, but never too
controversial.

You will always be in our heart and in our mind.

You join a list of talented artists that we had to leave behind.

We are sure you all will have a huge concert above.

Moreover, you all will continue to spread love.

Your music will continue to live on.

It will play on as if you had never gone.

You are the "King of Pop," but to many of us you were like a brother or friend.

These are, "Thoughts of Michael Jackson: A Musical Icon and Legend."

WHITNEY HOUSTON: WOMAN WITH A GOLDEN VOICE

Whitney Houston, we thank you for your contributions to the music industry.

If you had not set the bar so high, where would we be?

You had the most beautiful voice of our time.

I am expressing my condolences with these poetic lines that rhyme.

We remember you today in a positive light.

Any other way just wouldn't be right.

You were able to completely change the way we listened to music.

Knowing you're gone so soon makes us want to lose it.

We all anticipated your great comeback.

When it came to vocal talent you were ahead of the pack.

We all wanted to see you rise back to the top.

At least the playing of your songs will never stop.

You blessed us with an unforgettable rendition of the National Anthem.

It was played around the world again and again.

You inspired so many women to emulate you and step up their game.

Without you at the top things just won't be the same.

You join a list of talented artists who left us too soon.

You shot for the sky but were able to reach the moon.

You started in the church and made so many rejoice.

You will always be known as "Whitney Houston: woman with a golden voice."

GONE TOO SOON - THE ARTIST KNOWN AS PRINCE

I write this poem with a heavy heart.
Where do I begin? How do I start?
But I will write these lines that flow and rhyme.
For one of the greatest entertainers of our time.

It's all so surreal and somewhat insane.
It seems like yesterday we grooved to "Purple Rain."
A musical genius who left too soon.
I look towards the sky and see a purple moon.

Not just the sky but the heavens above.
He made us dance, sing, cry and even make love.
It brings sadness just to know you're gone.
However, your music and albums will play on and on.

You paved the way for so many artists of today.

You touched each one of us in some kind of way.

Your musical talent was such an inspiration.

It will continue to live from generation to generation.

People would line up to see you for blocks and blocks.

Your final performance was right here at Atlanta's Fox.

Your untimely death will never make sense.

You're "Gone too soon" and you're "The Artist known as Prince."

YOU ARE STILL THE GREATEST

You were known around the world as Muhammad Ali
A boxer who floated like a butterfly and stung like a bee
You were one of the most colorful boxers of our time
You would predict the knockout round and hit 'em with a rhyme.

You could wear them down with your "roper dope"
After ten or twelve rounds they had no hope
Let's not forget about your Ali shuffle
The "Thriller in Manilla" was not just a scuffle

You represented the way so many of us want to be
You heard it in our voices when we yelled, "Ali"
You were not just a great fighter but also a great man
I grew up watching you and was your biggest fan

When it came to boxing you were considered the king
But you accomplished so much outside the ring
You fought for equality for all mankind
Your kind of diligence is hard to find

Born in Louisville, Kentucky as Cassius Clay
"I am the greatest!" We would hear you say
It's sad your gone but here is the latest
We can all agree, "You are still the greatest."

KOBE BRYANT - MOST VALUABLE PLAYER

You created so many highlight reels
It's hard to express how everyone feels
You were special on and off the court
One of the best to ever play the sport

It was a horrible and shocking news flash
"Kobe Byant dies in a helicopter crash"
It's a day we will never forget
You were so young, and your life was pretty much set

I could discuss all your many accolades
It's the memory of you that I hope never fades
You grew up in the NBA
We all used to say, "Damn he can play!'

You were a player who changed the game
The Staples Center and LA will never be the same
You made every player around you greater
You always strived to be the best Laker

Sad thing is you went with your daughter.
It’s hard to believe that it could be divine order
For you and your family we'll all say a prayer
You're "Kobe Bryant - Most valuable player"

CONGRESSMAN JOHN LEWIS - A CIVIL RIGHTS ICON

I write this poem for the late, great Congressman John Lewis

I hear his voice, and I am compelled to do this

A notable legend for the civil rights movement

Your years in the fight were years well spent

You fought for equality for all mankind

A more noble endeavor is hard to find

There were so many ways that you inspired us

Far too many for me to discuss

We will never forget "Bloody Sunday"

You never let a beating stand in your way

You bravely marched across the Edmund Pettus Bridge

On the other side there would be beatings and carnage

Thirty-three years in the United States Congress
Georgia's Fifth District thanks you for your service
You gave the silent and voiceless a voice
Getting into "Good trouble" was never a hard choice

We remember your "March on Washington" speech
You were quite young but didn't hesitate to teach
We remember the marches, sit-ins, and protests
Less we forget your forty-something arrests

You did so much in the fight for equal rights
It turned out to be just one of your fights
So, go ahead and rest in peace
Our tenacity in the fight will never cease

You passed the torch so other generations can march on
You're forever, "Congressman John Lewis, a civil rights icon."

"TO YOU MOMMA WITH LOVE"

You have always been there for me.

You have always been strong because you needed to be.

So, since today is your special day.

I just have a few things that I need to say.

I remember the nights that you tucked me in.

You would say a prayer with me and kiss me with a grin.

You taught me to get an education and believe in myself.

You kept lots of powerful books in my room shelf.

I remember those cold mornings you took me to school.

Getting an education was your golden rule.

I remember the hours you spent helping me with my homework.

I am so glad that I did not drive you berserk!

Even though we had little and were pretty much poor.
You always made me feel like I had a whole lot more.
You always made sure I had a roof over my head.
I had plenty of clothes and a comfortable bed.

You always made sure I never missed a meal.
You just don't know how special you made me feel.
There were times when you got very little sleep.
On many occasions, I would even hear you weep.

You told me that some day I would be a strong man.
You taught me not to say, "I can't" but always say "I can."
I just wanted you to know that you are appreciated.
I am where I am because you made sure I was educated.

Every day is a special day for you mother.
I asked myself, "With words, how can I express my love for her?"
So, for all your countless hours making sure I was well taken care of.
This poem is especially, "To you momma with love."

EXPRESSIONS OF LOVE FOR MY TWO GOOD FRIENDS

I just have a few things to say to you.
First, thank you for all you have done and for all you do.
Just knowing you has been such a pleasure.
The amount of happiness you bring is hard to measure.

I am wishing you a happy anniversary.
A lifetime of happiness is what I hope you both see.
It is so wonderful to witness your undying love.
Your dedication to one another and to our Lord above.

So, just continue being the wonderful people you are.
I can assure you that your blessings will never be far.
You exemplify what true love and commitment is all about.
You are a wonderful couple, of course with no doubt!

We have known each other for quite a while.
You both have shown a lot of class and style.
I just wanted to thank you for being who you are.
When it comes to friendship and realness, you have certainly raised the bar.

I feel as if you are now a part of my family.
And that I always have two strong people who will stand with me.
I know what message I am hoping this poem sends.
These are truly, "Expressions of love for my two good friends."

YES, WE CAN! OR CAN WE?

President Obama's campaign slogan was "Yes we can!"
However, to be able to, we must have a good plan.
He also had a strong message about change.
When you're asked what it will take, you look at me strange.

The change should start with how we think.
If we don't change our thinking our very existence is on the brink!
I always say we need more accountability.
Without it, there can be no unity or stability.

We have never stopped making excuses.
If we don't try and we fail, who really loses?
We still say, "It's the man who is holding us back!"
It's not the man; it's the education we lack.

We still don't believe that education is key.
And with it, we can be whatever we want to be.
We still walk around with our pants hanging low.
I often wonder if this style will ever go!

We continue to sell drugs in our own communities.
Drug abuse in our neighborhoods is like an infectious disease.
Teen pregnancy is still a problem that needs to be addressed.
It's not condom use it's abstinence that should be stressed!

We still have fathers, who abandon their children.
I may find it necessary to reiterate this point again.
We continue to hang on the corner wasting time and drinking.
We can't get ahead like that, so what are we thinking?

We have never stopped wiping each other out.
Murder and violence has never been a good route.
There is still a disproportionate amount of us incarcerated.
Some of the causes for this have already been stated.

I am not trying to be judgmental or negative.

However, the change starts with what we do and how we live.

If we continue to do the same thing, we will get the same result.

Stop blaming everyone else when it's actually your own fault!

Whether we can or not is what we all wait to see.

I may sound skeptical, but I still say, "Yes we can! Or can we?"

EXPRESSIONS TO A SINGLE FATHER ON HIS SPECIAL DAY

I just have a few things I want to say.
I will start by wishing you a wonderful Father's Day!
I have known you for quite a while.
When I think of the times we had, I just have to smile.

I want to keep this short, but I don't know where to begin.
You have been there for your children through thick and thin.
You exemplify what a good father is all about.
You are one of the best fathers I know, and I have no doubt!

Even though it is hard to find good fathers in our communities.
The good ones are the ones that nobody acknowledges or sees.
I am proud to be able to call you my friend.
You are a good father in which your children can depend.

I know single parenthood and raising children is not always easy.

However, knowing there are good fathers like you around will always

please me.

You are a good man, father and friend is mainly what I wanted to say.

These are very sincerely, "Expressions to a single father on his

special day."

TO MY BABY WITH LOVE

I feel so blessed to have you in my life.
Perhaps someday you will become my first wife.
You have been there for the good times and the bad.
You always make me smile, even when I am sad.

You are that good woman, who is behind her good man.
To love, honor and cherish you is definitely the plan.
I am telling you how I feel on our anniversary day.
We will spend many more together; at least I hope and pray.

When you are with me I am such a happy person.
When you are not around my anxiety seems to worsen.
My heart still flutters when you come through the door.
It happens more often now than it ever has before.

When we are together, it is very much like magic.
If I ever lost you, it would definitely be tragic.
Even when you are not around you occupy my mind.
Without you at my side, I feel as if I am blind!

So as I sit here thinking about all the wonderful times.
I am expressing my feelings for you with this poetry that rhymes.
Finding you meant my prayers were answered by the good Lord above.
These feelings are very sincerely, "To my baby with love."

TO MY WIFE WITH LOVE

I just have a few things I want to say.

When I think of you so many feelings come to play.

I have known you for quite a while.

When I think of the times we have, I just begin to smile.

I want to keep this short, but I don't know where to begin.

You have been there for me and the children through thick and thin.

I feel so blessed to have you in my life.

It has been such a pleasure to have you as my wife.

You have been there for the good times and the bad.

You always make me smile, even when I am sad.

You are that good woman, who is behind her good man.

To love, honor and cherish you has always been my plan.

I am telling you how I feel in my own special way.
We will be together forever as long as we pray.
When you are with me, I am such a happy person.
When you are not around my anxiety seems to worsen.

My heart still flutters when you come through the door.
It happens more often now than it ever has before.
When we are together, it is very much like magic.
If I ever lost you, it would definitely be tragic.

Even when I am sick you nurse me back to health.
Having you there for me has been better than wealth.
Even when you are not around you occupy my mind.
Without you at my side, I feel as if I am blind!

So as I sit here thinking about all the wonderful times.
I am expressing my feelings for you with this poetry that rhymes.
Finding you meant my prayers were answered by the good Lord above.
These feelings are very sincerely, "To my wife with love."

BIRDS IN FLIGHT

I see so many birds flying high.
Sometimes it seems as if they take over the sky.
There are so many species of birds.
They are so beautiful it is often hard to put in words.

They all seem to have their own personalities.
I watch them as they soar high above the trees.
They soar through the air so gracefully and effortlessly.
Their Ariel acrobats are just so amazing to see.

They come in so many different shapes, sizes and colors.
They act like families with their parents, sisters and brothers.
Perhaps humans can learn from these beautiful creatures.
Sometimes animals and nature are our greatest teachers.

To watch them is such a beautiful sight.
Do yourself a favor and take the time to observe the "Birds in flight."

WHEN THE LIGHTS FADE AND THE CLAPPING STOPS

You did what it took to get you to the top.
You were determined, focused and would never stop.
You were definitely one of the best in the game.
However, you had an extremely tough rise to fame.

You came from deep in the heart of the inner-city ghetto.
There were times when you could have just given up and let go.
Your beautiful voice was your ticket out of the hood.
The fact that you never gave up turned out to be good.

You had what it took to stay on top for quite a while.
Few could even come close to duplicating your style.
Your music and lyrics were arguably the best.
Your high-powered performances separated you from the rest.

Many of your records topped the music charts.

You were always on your fans' minds and in your fans' hearts.

Suddenly, you are not so popular anymore.

Your music is no longer on the shelf of any store.

You can no longer even make the music charts.

This is actually when your biggest problem starts.

Your ratings have taken a major dive.

It is extremely difficult for you to thrive.

For you, getting to the top was a big issue.

However, when you fall nobody seems to really care or miss you.

Just like many Artists from the disco era.

Once upon a time, they lit up the charts and were quite a terror.

It is never easy when an artist rises to the top and then drops.

Moreover, "When the lights fade and the clapping stops."

BREAKING THE SPIRIT OF AVERAGE

It is a concept by Joseph B. Washington.
A notable speaker who gets the job done.
Inspiring you to be your very best.
Staying above average is your greatest test.

There are seven keys to breaking the spirit.
We should embrace this knowledge and never fear it.
The first key discusses your overall attitude.
It is what people remember so don't be so rude!

The second key discusses effective use of your time.
You can lose track of it at a drop of a dime.
The third key is to find good Mentors and Leaders.
Many of them are our greatest achievers.

The fourth key is to continue educating yourself.

There are so many good books on the store shelf.

The fifth key is to stay ahead of your opponents and opposition.

Even Haters have an agenda and mission!

The sixth key teaches you to set and accomplish goals.

It can help many of us to establish our roles.

The seventh key discusses empowering your belief system.

Many people give up when things get hard for them.

These seven keys can even help your marriage.

You can achieve anything by, "Breaking the spirit of average."

"DADDY DOESN'T LIVE HERE"

Daddy, I am sad that I never got to know you.

You walked out of my life before I turned two.

I wondered why you would abandon your son.

Growing up without you has not been fun.

Momma said, "Son I will always do the best I can.

But it won't be easy turning you from a boy into a man."

I never went to bed hungry.

Momma always made sure I was nice and comfy.

She is the main reason I managed to do so well.

If she ever doubted me, I could never tell.

But there are so many things I missed out on.

I needed your unconditional love, but sadly you were gone.

I needed you to teach me so much.
Without you I felt somewhat lost and a little out of touch.
Basically, I just needed you to be there.
If for no other reason, just to show me you care.

There was a time when I was extremely angry.
It just seemed like nobody could understand me.
With no role model, I nearly was lured into destructive behavior.
My desire to be successful just happened to be greater.

When I was a little boy momma made one thing clear.
By reminding me repeatedly, “Daddy doesn't live here.”

TOUGH DECISIONS STRONG LEADERSHIP:

A NATION DIVIDED

President Obama warned us that things would get tough.
Yet he was blamed both for doing too much and not doing enough.
We all know he did not get us into this mess.
That's something even the Republicans have to confess.

He is trying to bring this country through a tough recession.
We have all had to learn a very valuable lesson.
President Obama is keeping his promise of change.
Why are so many people acting so strange?

I am not surprised by his overall rating.
Perhaps it's not his policies but his race some are hating.
It is okay to disagree with the President and his policies.
But try doing it without all the hatred and violence please!

In this country change has never come easy.

But if it weren't for change, where would we be?

He has barely been President for more than a year.

Yet folks are twisting his agenda and thus spreading fear.

Some people have called the President a Socialist.

They feel he is spreading the wealth and it has them quite pissed.

Being the President requires, “Tough decisions and strong leadership.”

Some want him to fail and to send him on a one-way trip.

With his leadership the very fate of our nation can be decided.

Therefore, it's not unusual for it to lead to, “A nation divided.”

"I AM TRAYVON!"

He was killed in cold blood by George Zimmerman

An unarmed young black man shot down again

He claims he did it in self defense

After hearing the tapes, he made no sense

It is clear to us all that this is a homicide

He should turn himself in and stop trying to hide

Protected by a "Stand your ground" law

We all now know that it has a huge flaw

Florida Law enforcement failed to do an investigation

It has caused a lot of anger all over this nation

Justice Department it is now up to you

We are all waiting to see what you will do

The world is now behind Trayvon and his family

Justice will be served please understand me

We will make sure his death is not in vain

Only justice can ease his family's pain

We will accomplish this by peaceful demonstrations

Until there is justice, they will hear our frustrations

It's just so sad that he is now gone

But I am part of this movement and "I am Trayvon."

TAKEN TOO SOON: STUDENTS & TEACHERS OF SANDY HOOK

I write these words with a heavy heart
This senseless tragedy has torn us apart
So many youth lost in this tragedy
Protecting our youth is our most challenging strategy

Teachers and first responders you are also on our mind
Your heroism and selfless acts make you one of a kind
Because of you many children are still alive
We hope they get over this and we hope that they thrive.

We all struggle for answers about this terrible act
And with the fact that twenty-seven people will never come back
The entire nation feels your grief
I have no poetic words that will bring you relief

The whole nation stands behind you
In times of tragedy, it's simply what we do
Parents we know you are broken-hearted
Your healing from this tragedy has barely started

On how we stop these tragedies the nation is divided
But for better laws to protect us we are all united
The worst elementary school tragedy in our history
How it could happen is still a mystery.

However, the innocent lives lost will not be in vain
We shall continue to support you and share your pain
Schools across this nation will now have a safer look
You were "taken too soon, students and teachers of Sandy Hook"

"YOU SHALL SURVIVE"

You were born and raised deep in the heart of the inner-city.
You faced many challenges and never received pity.
You never had the opportunity to know your father.
You initially sought closure but later said, "Why bother?"

You were a domestic violence victim with very little hope.
Your desire to be free is what helped you to cope.
You were verbally and physically abused as a child.
The things you experienced were both scary and wild.

You were a rape victim with emotional distress.
There was no closure when the suspect decided to confess.
The poor economy has made things extremely hard.
Losing your job sort of caught you off guard.

You are a single mother with several mouths to feed.
You lacked education so it was hard to succeed.
You are a convicted felon trying to start over and find a job.
Your life became quite difficult when you decided to rob.

Nobody is perfect and we all make mistakes.
They strengthen us and tell us if we have what it takes.
You often wondered if your life could get any worse.
You finally decided to put the Lord first.

You experienced so much in life, yet you are still alive.
With the Lord in your life, "You shall survive."

ABOUT THE AUTHOR

Gary Tavares was born in New York on March 9, 1965. He faced difficult times when he and his five siblings were left without their parents. He was no older than four years old. They were all placed in a foster home in the Bronx, New York. The six of them stayed together, but the foster parents raised them. Their birth parents were never located.

Gary graduated from Evander Childs High School in the Bronx, New York, in 1983 at the age of eighteen. He served in the United States Navy from 1983 to 1986 and received an honorable discharge. He then joined the United States Army from 1986 to 1992 and was honorably discharged again.

In 1993, Gary discovered he had the gift of writing. He immediately began taking courses in creative writing to develop his newfound talent. Initially, it was a way to channel his energy and escape the realities of life. He later decided to use this gift to educate others and do something positive for his communities.

Gary started out writing educational plays. All four of his educational plays were produced on stage in California. He wrote, acted in, and directed each play. Additionally, he currently has four screenplays, including one that has won an award, a novel, an autobiography, an award-winning short film, and four poetry books, including this one.

Gary has used these educational and inspirational poems to reach out to the educational system and communities. In 2004, Gary became a Youth Motivational Speaker. He visits schools throughout the Atlanta, Georgia, area during career days and talks with students from grades four to twelve. The youth have shown overwhelming interest in Gary's educational and inspirational poetry.

Gary received an ink-pen signed "thank you" letter from President Obama and Michelle Obama. The letter was sent after Gary sent them a copy of his poem titled, **"From a Dream to a Reality: A Historic Election,"** which is included in this book.

In November 2005, Gary founded his own business in the Atlanta, Georgia, area. He is the CEO and founder of Tavares Entertainment, LLC. He offers creative and professional writing services, as well as the development of original works.

www.ingramcontent.com/pod-product-compliance
Lightning Source LLC
LaVergne TN
LVHW050600061026
849616LV00031B/354